Other People, Other Homes!

By Barry Milton

Pictures by John Lobben

Gareth Stevens Publishing
Milwaukee

BRIGHT IDEA BOOKS:

First Words!
Picture Dictionary!
Opposites!
Sounds!

The Four Seasons!
Pets and Animal Friends!
The Age of Dinosaurs!
Baby Animals!

Mouse Count!
Time!
Animal 1*2*3!
Animal ABC!

Homes Then and Now!
Other People, Other Homes!

Library of Congress Cataloging-in-Publication Data

Milton, Barry.
　　Other people, other homes!

　　(Bright idea books)
　　British ed. published as: Where do they live?
　　Bibliography: p.
　　Summary: Brief text and illustrations introduce the everyday life of
children in various countries around the world.
　　　1. Geography—Juvenile literature. 2. Children—Juvenile literature.
[1. Geography]
I. Lobben, John, ill. II. Title.
GN476.4.M57　1985　　　910　　　85-26256
ISBN 0-918831-62-8
ISBN 0-918831-61-X (lib. bdg.)

This North American edition first published in 1985 by

Gareth Stevens, Inc.
7221 West Green Tree Road　Milwaukee, Wisconsin 53223, USA

U.S. edition, this format, copyright © 1985
Supplementary text and illustration copyright © 1985 by Gareth Stevens, Inc.
Illustrations copyright © 1984 by Octopus Books Limited

First published as *Where Do They Live?* in the United Kingdom with an
original text copyright by Octopus Books Limited.

Typeset by Ries Graphics, Ltd.
Series Editors: MaryLee Knowlton and Mark J. Sachner
Cover Design: Gary Moseley
Additional Illustration: Thomas Shepherd
Reading Consultant: Kathleen A. Brau

Contents

United States of America

My name is Latoya. I live with my family in Chicago. Our building has apartments for twenty families.

After school, I play with my friends from the building. Sometimes we have to watc my younger brother while m parents work.

On Saturdays, I often go to the movies with my family.

In school, we do some of our lessons on computers.

Canada

My name is Marie. We live in Quebec, a French-speaking province in Canada. At school our lessons are in French and in English.

For almost half the year we have snow so deep that we travel on a snowmobile.

Often we go with our parents to Quebec City. In the evening we eat at a French restaurant. My favorite meal is steak cooked in red wine.

In the summer we vacation on one of Canada's many lakes. We like swimming and canoeing.

Mexico

My name is Carlos. We live in the south of Mexico. We grow corn, potatoes, melons, and red peppers and sell them at the local market.

In the evening my mother makes tortillas and fills them with vegetables or beans and meat.

Every Sunday we go to church. For special festivals, we carry a statue of the Virgin Mary through the streets.

Indians of the Americas

I am Little Mountain Flower of the Navajo tribe. I live in Arizona. My father is a logger in the forests owned by the Navajos.

The Navajo house is called a hogan. It is made of logs or stones covered with mud. Our brick house is a modern version.

My grandmother tells me the history of our tribe so I know where I came from. One day, I will tell my grandchildren.

To celebrate, we dress in traditional Indian clothes and dance and sing. Indians in Oregon and Washington make totem poles by carving figures of animals and birds into tree trunks.

Peru

My name is Maria. I live in a small village in Peru in the foothills of the Andes Mountains.

Most of our food comes from the beans, barley, and corn we grow. We make soup from beans and barley and grind corn into flour for bread.

We also keep sheep and goats.
Every day I take them up the
mountainside to eat the tall grass.

We use wool from the
sheep and goats to
make cloth. My mother
spins the wool, then
weaves it on her loom.

Eskimos

My name is Aliuk, and I live in the far north of Canada in a small wooden house. When my mother and father were young, they lived in an igloo, a house made of ice and snow.

In spring I hunt seals with my father. We travel across the ice on a sled pulled by a team of dogs called huskies.

We take the seal skins home and my mother dries and cleans them. We make them into warm clothes and blankets.

The traditional Eskimo way of life is changing, so we learn about our history at school.

Great Britain

My name is Barbara. I live in a village about 50 miles from London. In the center of the village is the village green.

Men play cricket on the green each Saturday. Every Sunday our family has a large midday meal. We often eat roast meat with potatoes.

Many young people in Great Britain enjoy horseback riding. I spend much of my spare time at the local riding school.

France

My name is Marcel. I come from a town in the south of France near the sea.

Many people in town work in hotels, shops, and restaurants. My father drives a taxi during the tourist season.

Every Sunday my grandparents join us for dinner. We usually finish our meal with a big fruit tart!

My father often takes me to the local café. We play a game called boules with heavy steel balls.

Switzerland

My name is Peter. I live in a village in the Swiss Alps. We travel on skis during the snowy winter.

After school and on weekends I meet my friends at a café. We drink hot chocolate or eat ice cream.

For most of the year the village is crowded with people on vacation. We enjoy showing visitors around the mountains.

During the summer, when the snow has disappeared, we play basketball and soccer.

Union of Soviet Socialist Republics

My name is Natalia. I live on a large farm 200 miles from Moscow. Twenty families live and work on the farm. We raise animals and grow wheat and corn to sell in Moscow.

My mother makes delicious pancakes, called blinis. We also eat vegetables, pickles, and eggs laid by the chickens we keep.

I go to a dancing class twice a week. Ballet is very popular in the U.S.S.R. I want to go to ballet school and learn to be a ballet dancer.

On weekends we go to the market in town to buy food and meet friends.

Australia

My name is Roy. I live on a sheep farm in South Australia. We have thousands of sheep.

The weather is hot all year round. When there is no rain for months, we use a windmill to pump water from a well.

The nearest town is hundreds of miles away, so I talk to my teacher by radio. All his students live on farms, and he broadcasts our lessons from a radio station!

Spring is the busiest time of the year. Sheep shearers come to the farm and cut off the sheep's thick winter coat, called fleece. The fleece is sent to a mill to be turned into wool.

Nigeria

My name is Babatunde. I live in a village in Nigeria, where we are all members of a tribe called the Yoruba.

My family raises vegetables, goats, and chickens for food. We also trade them for clothes and tools.

When the harvest is good, everyone celebrates. Men and boys wear large wooden masks. Long ago, people in our tribe wore the masks to scare off evil spirits.

Kenya

My name is Konchelah. My home is in Kenya, in East Africa. My family is part of the Maasai tribe. We move often to find new grazing land for our large herd of cattle. During the day, I help look after the cattle. At night we herd the cattle into a large area called a kraal.

We live in huts made of dried mud. I get up early in the morning to help my mother milk the cattle. We milk them again in the evening when they return from feeding.

India

My name is Shirin, and my home is in the south of India. We live in a house of brick and hard-baked clay.

Behind our house is a large yard. When the weather is really hot, we move our beds outside.

We go to school in the early morning, when it is still cool. Our lessons are in English and in Hindi, one of India's many languages.

My father grows wheat and corn on land just outside the village. Most farmers use animals to help them with their work. My father was the first person in our village to own a tractor!

Israel

My name
is Shimon.
I live on a kibbutz, a large farm
where many families live and work.

We grow flowers and
fruit to sell in town.
School gets out early
at harvest time so we
can help bring in
the crop.

We built all of the buildings ourselves. We have just finished a large hall to be used for meals and concerts.

For a special event like a wedding, everyone on the kibbutz celebrates. We sing and dance to traditional music.

Japan

My name is Koji, and this is my sister Michiko. Our family lives on a farm on Honshu, the main island of Japan.

Twice a week I go to a class where I learn Japanese fencing, called kendo.

I sleep on the floor on a mattress called a futon. In the morning I roll up the futon and store it till night.

My family grows rice in paddy fields. After we harvest it, we hang it to dry on wooden racks.

Norway

My name is Lars, and I live near the sea. My father is captain of a fishing boat and I help unload the cod, mackerel, and herring.

Winters are very cold in Norway. That is why our houses are built of wood, which keeps us warmer than brick or stone.

We keep a small herd of cows in the field next to our house. We also have a horse which pulls our sled during the winter.

At Christmas, we decorate our tree with real candles and sing traditional songs.

New Guinea

My name is Michael. The hills of New Guinea are covered by thick jungle. My village is in a jungle clearing.

Our longhouses are built on stilts to keep them dry during heavy rainstorms.

Every few months, we must cut down the plants that grow up around our village.

There are few roads through the jungle, so tools and medicine are brought to us by airplane.

For food, we pick
berries and mushrooms
and hunt for wild pigs
and birds.

美 People's Republic of China

My name is Mei, and I live in China. On the left you can see my name written in Chinese. In English it means "sister."

I live with my family on a commune. We look after farm animals and grow vegetables to eat and sell. We eat at a low table with chopsticks instead of knives and forks.

At school we study hard and learn to help each other on the commune.

The Chinese New Year is exciting. We have fireworks and carry a huge dragon through the streets.

Hawaii (U.S.A.)

My name is Joe. Hawaii is a state of the United States of America. It is a group of islands in the middle of the Pacific Ocean.

Outside of my town, most islanders live in small wooden huts. But the buildings in Honolulu are very modern.

People come from all over the world to surf in the big waves that roll into the beaches.

The weather in Hawaii is warm all year, so we always have fresh fruit. My favorites are melons and pineapples!

The following "Things to Talk About," "Fun Facts About Places," and "Things to Do" offer grown-ups suggestions for further activities and ideas for young readers of *Other People, Other Homes!*

Things to Talk About

1. Some of the children in this book live in homes with special names. Who might live in a hogan? in a longhouse? in an igloo? on a commune? on a kibbutz?

2. What foods do children from other places eat that you eat, too?

3. Children in Switzerland play basketball and soccer. Children in France play boules. Children in Hawaii surf. If you were to visit another land, what game or sport would you like to teach the children?

4. Which of the places in this book would you like to live in? Why? In what ways are these places like where you live now? How are they different? Do you think your parents would like to live there?

5. Which of the places would you like to visit?

Fun Facts About Places

1. There are about 4400 languages in the world. 850 of them are spoken in India!

2. On pages 6 and 7, we are told that French and English are both official languages of Canada. Many other countries have more than one official language. In Israel, both Arabic and Hebrew are official languages. And in tiny Switzerland, four languages are officially used: German, Italian, French, and Romansh, which is an ancient language related to Latin.

3. On Mt. Wai-'ale'ale in Hawaii, there are only six days out of the year when it does not rain.

4. The tallest building in the world is the Sears Tower in Chicago. Can you spot it in the Chicago skyline on pages 4 and 5?

5. The four countries with the largest area are the U.S.S.R., Canada, China, and the U.S.A.

6. The world's first city was near Jericho in what is now the Israeli-occupied West Bank. In 7800 B.C., 3,000 people lived there.

7. Only 10% of all the earth's land is farm land.

8. The oldest human fossils were found in Central Africa. They are 2 million years old.

9. The Himalayas of Asia are the highest group of mountains in the world. Mt. Everest, one of the Himalayas, is the earth's highest point.

10. 200 million years ago, the earth's land was only one continent. Africa and South America can be fit together like a puzzle along South America's east side and Africa's southwest side. Look at a map!

11. The crust of the earth contains 2,000 minerals. Industry uses only 100 of them.

Things to Do

1. In an atlas or dictionary or encyclopedia, look up the population of each country in this book.

2. Pick a country or culture that interests you. In your library, look for books that will tell you the answers to some of these questions:

   a. What language do the people speak?
   b. How are the children educated?
   c. What are some names people give to children?
   d. What kinds of things can children do when they grow up?
   e. Can both girls and boys do these things?

3. Children in many parts of the world need help. See if your teacher and classmates or your family can sponsor or help support a child who needs food, clothes, or other help. Think of things you and your friends can do.

4. Find an atlas or a map of the world with the names of countries and their major cities. Find these cities:

   a. Moscow
   b. Honolulu
   c. Paris
   d. Tokyo
   e. Peking
   f. Nairobi
   g. London

5. Invite someone you know from another country to visit your class to talk about his or her country. Prepare a list of interesting questions to ask.

6. See if your library has any books of stories from other lands or cultures. Find some that you like and read one to a younger friend or brother or sister. Draw a picture to illustrate part of the story.

More Books About Houses and Where Children Live

Here are some more books about houses and where children live. If you see any books you would like to read, see if your library or bookstore has them.

Anne Frank: Diary of a Young Girl. Frank (Pocket Books)

The Children's Book of Peoples of the World. Trundle (Usborne-Hayes)

The Days of the Cave People. Lebrun (Silver Burdett)

Desert Is Theirs. Baylor (Atheneum)

Dollhouse Magic: How to Make and Find Simple Dollhouse Furniture. Roche (Dial)

Dolphin Island: Story of the People of the Sea. Clarke (Berkeley)

Encyclopedia of the World and Its People (Bay Books)

A Home. Larsson (Putnam's)

Homes and Cities. Moorcraft (Franklin Watt)

Homes Then and Now! Mitchell (Gareth Stevens)

House Is a House for Me. Hoberman (Penguin)

Houses: Shelters from Prehistoric Times to Today. Siberell (Holt, Rinehart & Winston)

The Instant Answer Book of Countries. Warrender & Tyler (Usborne-Hayes)

My House. Scarry (Putnam's)

People. Spier (Doubleday)

Where Children Live. Allen (Prentice-Hall)

World of Tomorrow: Tomorrow's Home. Ardley (Franklin Watts)

For Grown-ups

Other People, Other Homes! is a picture book that introduces young readers to children from many countries and cultures. Vivid, charming illustrations and children's voices in clear prose portray simply and clearly the underlying variety — and reassuring similarity — of children's lifestyles throughout the world. Special activities further stimulate children's interest in the subject and in reading.

The editors invite interested adults to examine the sampling of reading level estimates below. Reading level estimates help adults decide what reading materials are appropriate for children at certain grade levels. These estimates are useful because they are usually based on syllable, word, and sentence counts — information that is taken from the text itself.

As useful as reading level scores are, however, we have not slavishly followed the dictates of readability formulas in our efforts to encourage young readers. Most reading specialists agree that reading skill is built on practice in reading, listening, speaking, and drawing meaning from language — activities that adults "do" when they read with children. These factors are not measured by readability scores; and yet they do enhance a text's value and appeal for children at early reading levels.

In *Other People, Other Homes!*, the "Contents," "Things to Talk About," "Fun Facts About Places," "Things to Do," and "More Books About Houses and Where Children Live" sections help children become good readers by encouraging them to use the words they read as conveyors of meaning, not as objects to be memorized. And these sections give adults a chance to participate in the learning — and fun — to be found in this book.

Reading level analysis: SPACHE 2.6, FRY 3, FLESCH 88 (easy), RAYGOR 3.5, FOG 6, SMOG 3